LIVE FREE JOURNEY : SMALL GROUP STUDY

JOHN 8:36 // JAN KERN

VE FREE JOURNEY: SMALL GROUP STUDY

A LIVE FREE RESOURCE

Standard®
PUBLISHING

Cincinnati, Ohio

Published by Standard Publishing, Cincinnati, Ohio
www.standardpub.com

Live Free books also available: *Scars That Wound : Scars That Heal, Seduced by Sex : Saved by Love*, and *Eyes Online : Eyes On Life*

Printed in the United States of America

Project editors: Lindsey Holder, Robert Irvin
Cover design: Scott Ryan
Interior design: Edward Willis Group, Inc.

Published in association with the Books & Such Literary Agency, 52 Mission Circle, Suite 122, PMB 170, Santa Rosa, CA 95409-5370, www.booksandsuch.biz.

ISBN 978-0-7847-2361-6

15 14 13 12 11 10 09   1 2 3 4 5 6 7 8 9

CONTENTS

DEEPER, FULLER, FREER

Maybe life has gotten pretty rough around the edges. Maybe at times it seems downright impossible. Pressures and circumstances press in. Choices—those made by yourself or others—have turned into traps and painful consequences. Where does that leave your story? With pages you wish you could tear out and tear up? With future pages that seem destined to be bleak?

Through *Live Free Journey : Small Group Study* you'll have the opportunity to look honestly at those pages—but you're going to see real possibilities that they can be filled with a fresh hope and a future beyond anything you might imagine today. You'll discover a connection with God that's more personal than you've known before, one that begins to heal the hurts of the past and takes you forward with greater strength to face the tough moments ahead. You'll begin to see how God personally meets you and offers an invitation to take your own Live Free journey.

Of course, a lot of that is up to you. But the more you put yourself into the experience of seeking to live free, as God intends you to, the more you'll learn about yourself and God in life-transforming ways.

At the beginning of each *Live Free Journey* session, in "Prepare to Connect," you're offered ways to get ready to meet as a group. Take some time to follow the preparation suggestions and read through the first half of the study before you get together. As a group each week, you'll begin to get to know each other and share more of your personal stories, questions, and challenges—all as you work through the questions and activities under "Together."

Following each session you can take what you've learned or talked about to a more personal level through "Just You and God." Try either working through all the "A Look Inside" questions the next day after the group meets, or answer a question each day throughout the week. "A Step Deeper" offers ways to take what you're discovering and use it in practical and consistent ways in your life, deepening your relationship with God. Bottom line: there is a lot of material in this book. Don't feel compelled to have to work through every point and every verse.

You'll notice in the first session that there are a few questions to encourage you to work together to create a safe place where everybody can share stories, questions, and struggles with their journeys. Commit to keeping what is shared within the group confidential, and look for ways to be supportive of each other.

In many cases, it will be best that your small groups are kept as gender-exclusive—guys with guys and girls with girls. Some of the sessions may go very deep—and this is a separation that will be necessary. Your ministry or parachurch leader will guide that direction in your groups.

Within the studies you'll also get to know real people with real stories. Their stories show how God helped them take the courageous steps needed to overcome their deep hurts and traps.

You'll meet:

✦ Jackie, in session one, Journey: Jackie's story is told more fully in the Live Free book *Scars That Wound : Scars That Heal—A Journey Out of Self-Injury*. With arms marked with countless cuts and emotional scars that slashed across her heart, Jackie felt defeated. She never thought she could live a life free from the anxiety and pain that led to her self-destructive choices. But Jackie began to feel hope when God brought people into her life to help her discover the journey of hope and freedom he had for her.

• Mike, in session two, Story: By eight years old, life was already tough for Mike. His father committed suicide. In Mike's mind, his father chose to abandon his family, and Mike felt he wasn't worth sticking around for. Unfortunately, the ache of the loss and lack of value stuck around. As a teen these feelings would nudge Mike toward increasingly more destructive choices and traps, including stealing, drinking, and gang involvement. But then he found others who cared about his story, who cared about him. And he discovered God did too.

• Suzy, in session three, Connection: More of Suzy's story unfolds in the book *Seduced By Sex : Saved By Love—A Journey Out of False Intimacy*. By the time Suzy stepped into high school, she had a plan: shed any goodie-goodie image and do whatever it takes to get in with the cool crowd, even if that meant giving herself away—over and over. And Suzy's life didn't get better. She spiraled into a hopeless lifestyle that she didn't know how to escape. In her mind, she couldn't turn to God because he couldn't possibly want anything to do with her. Healthy connections with others brought about a different conclusion, and she found a God who not only loved her but who was also pursuing her.

Suzy's story is also featured in session six, Deeper Still.

• Colin, in session four, Freedom: Colin's story is found in *Eyes Online : Eyes On Life—A Journey Out of Online Addictions*. Hopeless, lonely, and depressed, Colin gravitated to the place he felt most comfortable—the Internet. Disappointments, hurts, and depression drew him deeper and deeper to obsessions that included surfing, gaming, and porn. But with God and with others, Colin found a way out and discovered he could have a life of purpose and real-world relationships.

• Tiffany, in session five, Going Deeper: Tiffany loved her father, but then he committed one of the greatest betrayals: he sexually molested her. By the time she was a teen, Tiffany saw herself as trash. Her self-hatred became her biggest battle and exhibited itself in the beginnings of an eating disorder, excessive exercise, and self-injury. It was at church that she found solid friendships, especially in her youth pastor's wife, that offered the opportunities to tell her story and to get to know deeply the God who saw her as someone beautiful and loved.

Besides Jackie, Mike, Suzy, Colin, and Tiffany, you'll meet others interviewed for the Live Free series of books or for this resource, young people like Cory, Justin, and Katie. You might relate to some of their stories. Watch for their thoughts and insights throughout the studies.

While you work through the pages of this study and the pages of your own story, I invite you to visit www.choose2livefree.com, where you can find more information and resources to encourage you to continue your own Live Free journey.

Ready to go deeper, fuller, freer? Begin by praying—honestly, at a gut level—to God. Tell him where you are right now and what you most hope for. Then turn the page and begin to take the journey with him, and others, that can change your life forever.

> May you experience the love of Christ,
> though it is too great to understand fully.
> Then you will be made complete with all the
> fullness of life and power that comes from God.
> EPHESIANS 3:19, NLT

one journey

- Spend some time reading about Peter's life. Use the Scriptures included throughout this session and under "Journey Transformations."
- Read "Experience It" (page 19) and bring two pictures to the first session—one representing where you are right now in your journey and the other where you'd like to be someday.

Leader note: Have extra pictures on hand for newcomers who might not have had time to prepare.

YOU MET JACKIE in the introduction. She had cut and burned herself and then also tried using drugs, drinking, and having sex with guys to block waves of emotion and pain. She didn't like how she felt inside or where her life was headed. Would it ever be any different? Could God help her? Could God even *like* her? Jackie wasn't sure.

As she became more involved in the youth group at her church, she felt the heaviness of the contrast of her life in comparison to those around her. She struggled with thoughts that she was bad, that she didn't deserve to have God's love or a life that played out any differently or any better than the constant pain in which she lived.

> *The prayer time Jackie had experienced the week before was genuine. God's presence was real. But the emotions inside still crashed like waves against all that felt wrong in her life.*
> (Scars That Wound : Scars That Heal, p. 46)

Journeys.

Disappointment, pain, fulfillment. Choices, traps. Victories, setbacks. Unexpected paths.

Descriptions of a life in process. If you were to choose one of those words as being most like your life right now, which would it be?

How about what you most hope for? Would you choose one of those words? Or would you choose another?

Does what you hope for feel out of reach? Like something that, if you caught hold of it, would disappear like vapor in your hand? It doesn't have to. Not when you connect it to a relationship with God. The freedom, life, and hope he offers are real and lasting. Nothing else comes close.

Jesus said to the people of his time, "My purpose is to give [you] a rich and satisfying life" (John 10:10, *NLT*). And, "If the Son sets you free, you are truly free" (John 8:36, *NLT*).

Those messages are for each of us too. Today. Right now. Take a moment to take that in—Jesus is speaking to you personally. What would it take for you to let Jesus' words impact your life, to change it forever?

It's not an easy question. But it's worth considering such a journey—especially when it means experiencing a deeper place with God than you've ever imagined. Even when it means he sees *all* of who you are.

MARIUS became addicted to Internet gaming. Hours and hours online each day left no time for connecting to life and relationships or for discovering the full journey God had in mind for him.

"God started to show how meaningless it all was—how pursuing gaming had no true fulfillment," he said. "That it would ultimately destroy me, and that instead God had abundant life for me."

As a young Christian, ERICKA became depressed and began to cut herself. The harsh judgment of others made her doubt God's willingness to love or help her. She said:

"For a while I was frustrated with religion. I was terrified of Jesus but not mad at him. I thought my sins were so bad, I was a monstrosity. I hoped Jesus didn't see me as a bad girl that needed to be punished."

It took some time for Ericka to realize that Jesus wanted her to fully experience his hope and freedom. Today she can say, "I knew God would pull me through. His promises never fail."

Meet a guy named Simon Peter. He was, in many ways—like Jackie, like you and your friends—an ordinary guy. Far from perfect. Peter had already met Jesus by the Galilean Sea but had only a partial clue of who this man was. After one long, pathetic night of fishing, Peter and his buddies cleaned their nets and got ready to head home. (Read Luke 5:1-11.)

Then Jesus showed up. First he asked some fishermen to take him out onto the lake so he could use their boat as a teaching platform for the crowd gathering on shore. After Jesus finished speaking, he invited Peter and the guys to go fishing again. They'd been after it the entire night before—with no luck. But they took Jesus at his word, lowered their nets, gave it some time, and this time they caught fish—so many that the catch almost sank their boats.

In that moment, something else happened. Peter caught a glimpse of Jesus as God in the flesh. Though he didn't fully get what that meant, he was aware of the contrast of the holiness of the person standing before him and the exposed shame and need of his own soul. Peter fell to his knees in front of Jesus and said, "Oh, Lord, please leave me—I'm too much of a sinner to be around you" (Luke 5:8, *NLT*).

That reaction is natural—what any of us might do when we realize *all* of our secrets, *all* of who we really are, is laid bare before a holy God. Peter wanted to send Jesus away. Jesus didn't go. Instead he invited Peter to join him in a journey, one that would require much courage.

Peter, by the way, is the name Jesus chose to call him. It means "rock" (Matthew 4:18; John 1:42; Matthew 16:18). The name fit. Sort of. Peter was devoted, faithful, confident, energetic. He was a leader. At first, those strengths played out more like someone driving a truck with a 454 engine—but with lousy reach of the pedals and little ability to handle the gearshift. Peter had some growing to do. Jesus knew that and didn't mind. He saw who Peter could become.

Over the next three years, Peter followed Jesus through the countryside, ate with him, prayed with him, learned from him, served others with him. An amazing experience, but it was also tough. Peter wrestled with understanding who Jesus was and why he came. A few stops along his journey show that he said things and made choices that revealed his own weaknesses, traps, and failings.

Walking across a stormy sea toward Jesus, Peter wavered between bold faith and doubt (Matthew 14:27-31). Other times you see him tell Jesus what he should or shouldn't do (John 13:8, 9; Matthew 16:21-23), wrestle with forgiveness (Matthew 18:21), push for recognition (Matthew 19:27), or react rashly (John 18:10, 11). He declared his loyalty to the death and then, after Jesus was arrested, at his lowest point, Peter denied any connection to him three times (John 13:37, 38; 18:15-18, 25-27). Later the risen Jesus restored their relationship as Peter, in three statements, reaffirmed his love for him (John 21:15-17).

But Peter also became a leader of the early church and powerfully testified in his first

KEVIN and AMANDA, once entirely committed to saving sex for marriage, let one compromise lead to another. First they gave in and broke God's standard in their own relationship. Sex with others followed, as did much brokenness and pain. They felt ashamed and hopeless. But good friends were there to help them see God hadn't given up on them.

"Despite everything we went through, we realized God never left or changed," Kevin said. "He was there waiting for us. We needed to be willing to return to him."

public message, at Pentecost, exactly who Jesus was: God's Son. Three thousand people were saved after Peter preached Jesus as Lord for the first time (Acts 2:14-41)! He stood firm in the face of criticism and scrutiny from the religious community. He endured persecution and imprisonment, and eventually, according to historical accounts, suffered his own crucifixion upside down—because he felt unworthy to die as his Lord had.

As Peter pushed forward into all Jesus called him to be, his journey formed him into "the rock"—just as Jesus knew it would. In the letters that Peter wrote later in his life (1 Peter and 2 Peter), you see his radical transformation.

Your own journey is filled with choices, pushing through your weaknesses to discover the strengths Jesus sees in you, overcoming traps and setbacks, traveling along unexpected paths, and experiencing a mix of disappointment and fulfillment. Life in process. Learning, discovering, and growing through the courageous journey Jesus invites you to take.

He'll walk with you there. He doesn't promise a life without expectations, pressures, or traps, or without the difficult choices you need to make every day. He *does* offer a relationship that will help you through and a freedom that will bring purpose and hope to your story, to your journey.

Over the next few weeks, you'll begin that journey. You'll have a few things to consider and talk through, some choices to make. Look around you. Like Peter, you won't take your journey alone. You have traveling companions. Most of all, if you choose, you have Jesus. A relationship with him will make this a journey you'll never forget.

Jackie began to discover that too. God met her in her darkest moments of self-injury and self-loathing and began to answer her deepest questions. He sent others to come alongside Jackie to encourage her and to help her know him. She found a God who loved her beyond anything she could imagine, who had in mind for her an amazing journey of hope, freedom, and transformation.

The warm August night was filled with the sounds of bullfrogs and crickets. One small lamp lit the steps where Jackie and Sue sat down to pray.

Sue pushed her hands into her dark blue sweatshirt and turned toward Jackie. "I think we can help each other. Your cutting and my eating problems—they're what we go to in our darkest moments. Maybe we can figure out a better way to deal with things."

(Scars That Wound : Scars That Heal, p. 99)

I cry out to God Most High, to God, who will fulfill his purpose for me.

PSALM 57:2, NLT

TOGETHER

/ / Consider It

For Jackie, "life in process" meant having to face her pain. She did that through opening up to a young woman who became her friend at a ministry for at-risk youth; through meeting with two women, Judy and Stephanie, in their living room and listing her many painful relationships; through forgiving others and forgiving herself—and much more.

List words that describe "life in process" for you—things that may be complicated or simple.

Considering where you'd like your journey to go, what seems out of reach as you look at things today?

What things seem difficult—but possible?

Describe what freedom is to you. What is the freedom Jesus talked about when he said that if he sets you free "you are truly free"?

Talk about how Peter might have felt when God revealed himself in Jesus, and Peter became deeply aware of his own brokenness and sinfulness. What questions do you have right now about who Jesus is? When you've felt the heaviness of the contrast between yourself and the holiness of God, have you, like Peter, wanted to send Jesus away?

Jesus saw who Peter could become and who Jackie and others could become. He sees the possibilities for every person in this group. What possibilities do you think Jesus sees? Your small group leader may wish to facilitate open sharing in the group for a few minutes. If so, share your thoughts and possibilities with the rest of the group. (Note: remember to always keep things positive!)

Now that you've had some time together in this first session, consider these questions for your group in the weeks to come:

+ What will make this group a safe place to share and be completely real with each other?

+ What do you want to see happen in this group? What personal and group commitments do you need to talk about to help make those things happen?

JOURNEY TRANSFORMATIONS

Choose topics and verses below and talk about the journey transformation Peter experienced:

Not fully understanding who Jesus is:
Matthew 14:28; 16:22; 19:27; Luke 5:5-10; John 13:6-8, 37

Journey transformation: knowing him well:
Matthew 16:16; Luke 9:20; 1 Peter 2:25

What aspects of Jesus do you feel like you don't know well? What do you want to understand better?

Wanting recognition, reacting:
Matthew 16:21-23; 18:21; Mark 8:32; John 18:10, 11
Journey transformation: self-control, maturity, humility, and grace:
1 Peter 2:1, 2; 2:16-21; 5:5-7

What parallels to gaining self-control, maturity, humility, and grace do you see in your life?

Unaware of Satan's influence:
Matthew 16:22, 23
Journey transformation: encouraging others in watchfulness and firmness of faith:
Acts 5:3, 4; 1 Peter 5:8, 9

What are some practical ways you can be aware of Satan's schemes and move toward a more solid faith in Jesus?

Denying Christ:
Matthew 26:33-35, 69-75; John 13:37, 38; 18:15-18, 25-27
Journey transformation: defending Christ and being willing to suffer for his sake:
Acts 4:1-20; 12:1-5; 1 Peter 3:14-17; 4:12-19

Where do you see yourself needing to grow in boldness of faith?

Seeing his career of fishing as the limit of his life calling:
Matthew 4:18; John 21:3
Journey transformation: taking a journey of risky and courageous faith:
Acts 2:14; 3:12-26; 4:8-13, 19, 20; 5:29-32; 8:14; 9:34-40; 10:34, 35; 12:5-11; 15:7; 2 Peter 1:5-12

Recognize any limits you've set for yourself. Where might God take you in your journey of courageous faith?

/ / Experience It

Take out the two pictures you brought—one representing where you are right now in your journey and the other where you'd like to be someday.

As a group or in smaller groups or pairs, share your pictures. As you do, talk about your journey ahead, especially in light of God's plan for you and the healing and hope he wants for you.

Talk about how a journey is not just about what we're moving out of but what we're going toward. Use this as an opportunity to share how you can help and encourage each other. You can choose journey-type verses from the Bible that are meaningful to you.

JUST YOU AND GOD

/ / A Look Inside

Jesus saw Peter as someday becoming "the rock." And Peter did. Ask God to help you see what you can become. What words describe those possibilities for you? Write more about *why* you chose those words: how would that kind of person think, live, focus? What would their relationships look like?

What are your most difficult obstacles, addictions, or traps?

Your journey following Christ will take making some tough choices and commitments. Which choices will be easy for you? Which will be most difficult?

What will it take for you to make the commitment to your journey ahead? What will you do first?

Identify at least one person you can ask to be a support as you create and keep journey commitments. Commit to yourself that you will ask that person within the next couple of days for their help.

/ / A Step Deeper

Journeys need a plan, a destination. You might have one in mind, but living free, truly free, involves a destination shaped by God. Start a journal that you will use during these six sessions. Here are some thoughts on getting started:

+ Write what living free means to you personally.

+ Write out any of the answers that you wish to from the questions in the units in this book.

+ Write a prayer asking God to help you shape the journey ahead.

God was there, helping her take one step at a time, and he sent people to care and walk alongside Jackie. He would continue to be with her in the next stage of her journey.

(Scars That Wound : Scars That Heal, p. 89)

ON THE SIDE : JOURNALING

At the end of the session you just completed was a suggestion to begin a journal. It's entirely optional, but doing so for this study can give you a place to be honest with yourself and also a place to be hopeful as you trust God to lead your story and your journey.

Just as journaling is extremely personal, so is journaling style. You can write for pages and pages if you like, or just jot down a few thoughts, a prayer, or a quick list. You can also use your journal as a place to write out your thoughts and responses to questions in the study. Here are some more ideas:

• Write new insights as they come up during your small group meetings or at other times during the week.

• List questions that you'd like to ask about God and your relationship with him.

• Write prayers or notes to God as you think through the material in the sessions—or anytime during the next few weeks when you want to talk to him.

• Create songs, poetry, or sketches about God's pursuing love for you and what he's creating in your life.

• Write down words of encouragement or insight you've received from others in the group.

• List moments from your small group that make you laugh, smile, or think deeply—these are all gifts from God.

• Add new Bible verses as they become meaningful to you, especially relating to your journey toward deeper hope and freedom.

- Write out lyrics to worship songs so you have them available for your personal time with God.
- Draw or write sketches of the new identities that God is creating within you on your journey. Examples: beautifully and purposely created (Psalm 139:14); strong and courageous (Joshua 1:9); a child of light (Ephesians 5:8).
- Write notes as you listen to studies or sermons and then write thoughts and prayers about what you're learning.

- Use the space on this page and page 23 to get your journaling started.

two story

- Take time to think about your personal story and where God has entered the picture.
- Read Genesis 1:26–3:10.

Leader note: For the "Experience It" activity you will need small bricks that can be written on and stacked (enough for a foundation row that all the students in your small group can build on); three bricks for each member of your group; bold black marking pens.

WOVEN INTO OUR JOURNEYS are the unfolding pages of our personal story—how we've bumped up against life through our relationships, faith, questions, struggles, and choices.

The early pages of Mike's story included growing up in church and learning a lot about God. But for Mike, God was just something to know *about*, not *someone* to know in a personal relationship. Mike's early pages included tragedy when his father committed suicide. Feeling he didn't matter enough for his father to stick around led to a wavering sense of value for Mike. This feeling dropped him into a string of bad choices, one after another: smoking, drinking, shoplifting, doing poorly in school. Eventually, he joined a street gang.

He had hoped to find the acceptance and identity he was longing for. Instead he felt empty.

Think back to a time when a decent day eroded into one you wished you could erase forever. Life was OK, you were getting

> "I got into a lot of trouble. The worse the choices I made, the farther away from God I felt. I still believed the truth that God was God. But I thought he probably didn't approve of what I was doing, and that he was waiting for me to get my act together for us to be in a relationship and for him to love me. Honestly, I didn't want to do what I thought you had to in order to be in [a] relationship with God. I had to realize that I couldn't get to God by being good."
>
> —Mike

along fine—and then something happened that changed everything, especially you. Your perceptions of yourself, of others, even of God, shifted and splattered your world with confusion, anger, hurt, or sadness. What happened became a permanent page or chapter in your story, the bold, black ink seeming to overshadow early pages of promise, innocence, and good. Maybe you attempted to get past it, but any progress felt obscured by stalking memories of pain or regret, a feeling that you were on a collision course with hopelessness.

Intrusions, violations, or abandonment by others. Our own choices and traps. All these seem to engrave an inescapable groove into our lives. Is there hope in seemingly impossible circumstances? Is God there? And if he is, how do we shake the nagging feeling that he wouldn't want anything to do with us anyway?

When his parents told him he couldn't use their computer, NATE would sneak onto his friends' computers and spend hours messaging and looking up art and porn. He said: "I let go of all my morals just so I could wallow in my sinful nature. I felt ashamed and thought I must be a disgrace to God. He wouldn't want to look at me. I didn't believe he would help me with something like an online addiction. But he did. Now I pray and he's right there with me when I go online."

Step back in time—way back in time—to Adam and Eve. Take a look at their story—maybe in a way you never have before.

Drop down into the garden that God gave them. Walk with them through those beginning days. Imagine the beauty of their surroundings and the freedom and companionship they enjoyed with each other and with God. There was only one taboo, one simple tree to stay away from—the tree of the knowledge of good and evil. Eat the fruit of that one, God told Adam, and "you will surely die" (Genesis 2:15-17). A warning, but also a choice.

Initially that was probably cool. No problem. Plenty of other things to do, plenty of other places to be.

But slithering onto the scene came the serpent, the deceiver, Satan-in-disguise with words dripping with enticement. He would use his skill to break down their defenses, to eat away at their trust in God, their maker. He began with Eve.

"God told you not to eat from *any* tree?"

"No," Eve countered. "Just not from the one in the middle of the garden. Eat it, even touch it, we die." (Eve might have added the "no touching" part to God's warning.)

The serpent's hollow laughter filled the air. "Of course you can eat its fruit. God just knows that if you do, you'll be like him, knowing good and evil." (See Genesis 3:1-5.)

Hear the mockery, the enticement, the trap. Hear the lies.

It even seems possible the serpent might have led Eve to the very foot of the tree to see just how beautiful and tantalizing it was. Doubt slid into Eve's heart. *Maybe God doesn't have our best interests at heart. Maybe he's holding back.*

She believed the lie. She picked the fruit, took a bite, and then

Adam did too. At that instant, they felt and knew things they never imagined. But instead of the moment being filled with glorious delight in new knowledge, freedom, and power, it was irreversibly stained with shame. Now evil tainted what, a moment before, had seemed only good. Nakedness no longer felt natural and innocent. Dark and twisted thoughts—very unfamiliar thoughts—drove them to cover themselves (Genesis 3:6, 7).

The Bible only gives us a few words to describe these scenes, but they can't be passed over quickly. Behind them are events that altered the direction of history and brought about the struggling existence we know today.

But in the next words there is also hope.

Turn again to the story. In response to Adam and Eve's choice to go against his warnings, God did not hurl lightning bolts. Nor did he thunder through the garden smashing trees and shouting angry words of condemnation. It could be that that's what Adam and Eve expected, even deserved. Maybe what we'd expect. But this is how God's actions are described: He came "walking in the garden in the cool of the day" (Genesis 3:8). No thunderbolts or shouts. Yet Adam and Eve, now holding a distorted perception of God and completely drenched in understandable shame and regret, *hid*.

The impact of that is easy for us to miss: they hid from the living God.

STEPHANIE bought into the lies and the cheapened view of sex she saw in the movies and on TV. This only left her lost and empty. Then she discovered that God had a different story for her. Stephanie said: "I had to come to the end of myself, or at least who I thought I was, and abandon any resemblance to the 'old me.' I became a new creature in Christ. At first I was very uncomfortable and shaky. Over time, I've regained my self-confidence and am happy with the new me that God is creating."

After being released from the hospital for self-injury wounds, MARI sat in her darkened room wanting to cut herself again. With a dull paring knife she started to cut, but then she felt God telling her that he loved her no matter what. She stopped. "That profoundly affected my life," she says. "God is the lover of my soul. He never leaves. I have not cut since."

God asked a simple question: "Where are you?" (Genesis 3:9).

Now, he's God. He knew exactly where they were. And even though what they've done is painful—a decision that will impact their future existence and something they need to face—God's question is meant to go deeper than just a recounting of their choice.

"Where are you?"

Could that be a question coming from his own broken heart, now filled with the deepest grief you can imagine, most of all a longing to restore the relationship he once had with them? Could it be an invitation to come out of their place of hiding and shame to return to him?

Throughout the entire Bible, God's passionate pursuit of his own is clear. From Genesis to Revelation, we see the connecting threads of his desire to restore our relationship with him. His question "Where are you?" was the launch of that pursuit, and it is a question he asks each of us, especially in the darkest moments of our own stories.

Where are you?

Let's fast forward to another moment in time.

In John 4, Jesus meets a woman at a well outside the gates of Samaria. At the start of the story, we as readers and observers don't know much about this woman, but it's quickly clear that Jesus knows all about her. He knows her lifestyle, her many husbands, and her current relationship with someone she's not married to. He also knows the deepest needs of her heart, and it's her heart he's most interested in. He begins there, in fact, by offering "living water" (John 4:10-14)—God's continual and overflowing presence in her life. Jesus knows only this can transform the dry cracks of her life.

Though his exact words aren't "Where are you?", this is the question Jesus is asking as he leads the woman to reveal the whole truth of her story—not for him, but for *her*. Only when she recognizes, even admits, where she is in her story can she move forward to discover the hope he offers for a different life.

That's powerfully true for all of us. True for you. Where are you? What is the story you need to tell?

Mike's life smashed into a hard wall, and he sought help. At a ministry for at-risk teens, he watched how others lived and saw that Christianity was something vital and real. He began to believe God wanted a personal relationship with him no matter what Mike had done. He felt it—God loved him—and Mike began to sense the beginnings of freedom and hope.

That's what God does. He refuses to allow traps, pain, and darkness to be the last page of your story. With his question "Where are you?", he's inviting you to come out of hiding.

> "I was getting in trouble with reckless abandon. I didn't care what happened. But God never let me get too far from him. He was always there to draw me back. I was trying to get my identity and self-worth through these people who in the end made me feel empty, and I ended up searching for God and discovering I was an individual who he loves."
>
> —Mike

> For you were once darkness, but now you are
> light in the Lord. Live as children of light.
>
> Ephesians 5:8

TOGETHER

// Consider It

Considering Adam and Eve's story, talk about what might have been going on when they hid. In what ways does your story parallel theirs?

What difference does it make whether you keep God at a distance or hide and keep secrets about your choices, hurts, or traps?

Mike held on to some wrong perspectives that kept him from connecting with God for quite a while. What is something new you discovered about God through Adam and Eve's story? What old perspectives about God can you let go of—especially in relationship to your story and how you think he might respond?

Jesus knew the Samaritan woman's story. He knows ours. What does each of us gain by being willing to think through, face, and tell the whole truth of our story? What can you personally gain by telling yours?

Tell what you know about the threads and themes that hold all the way through the Bible, woven from Genesis to Revelation, that show God's pursuit to restore our relationship with him.

How does your story fit into God's bigger story? What does that tell you about your importance to God?

JOURNEY TRANSFORMATIONS

How you view your story impacts your journey. Explore some of the verses below to consider how your story can be amazing, hopeful, and filled with an experience of freedom and fullness.

Your story has an important place within the context of the huge story God has been unfolding since the beginning of time. Read through: Job 12:10; Psalm 139:15, 16; Acts 17:24-28

What have you discovered about your story that you didn't know before?

Though you live in the present, your story is unmistakably a part of not only a great history but also an amazing future—one beyond your imagination. Read: Jeremiah 29:11; Ephesians 3:20

What is one new hope you can have for your future, beginning today?

As much as your story sometimes seems entirely out of your control, it can be in God's loving and capable hands. Read: Psalm 37:4-7; Isaiah 41:10; Jeremiah 32:41

How does this change your view of God?

You are a main character in your story, and God sees you in very specific and hopeful ways. Read:
Genesis 1:27; Psalm 139:14; 2 Corinthians 5:17; Ephesians 2:10
How does this change your view of yourself?

// Experience It

Living out the story God is unfolding in you starts right where you are right now. Begin by talking about God's foundations for a great future. Write those ideas and any supporting verses on the foundation row of bricks (1 Corinthians 3:11; Hebrews 6:1; others). When you're finished, line those up on the floor or a table to create a bottom row to build on for the next step.

Next, each of you has three of your own bricks. You can build community with this activity, and make it even more powerful, by writing on your bricks:

+ a new direction you would like to see your life take

+ one specific commitment you're willing to make

+ one new way you'd like to bring God into your story more

+ your name or initials on a side where you've written

Now stack all the bricks on the foundation row.

Talk about how the foundation ideas will help you move forward in the story God has for you. If you choose to mix bricks from the different students when you stack them, you can also talk about how our stories intertwine with the stories of others and how God uses the body of Christ to encourage growth.

This activity also will lead into the next session, Connection.

When you're finished, you can choose to keep your bricks or, for more encouragement, trade or share them during the rest of the session.

JUST YOU AND GOD

/ / A Look Inside

How have the choices, traps, or events of your life impacted your perception of God and his love and concern for you? Do the stories of Adam and Eve, the woman at the well who talked with Jesus, or Mike help you grasp a deeper understanding that could help change that perception?

Write about the pages in your story that are most difficult for you. Consider which ones were completely out of your control and which ones involved choices you made.

Take a look at one page of your story that involved your choices; now consider future pages. What are you willing to do to change or improve the direction of your story? How can you start today?

Who can you share your story with and ask to help you?

/ / A Step Deeper

Think about your own story—past events and what's going on with you today. How would you answer God's question, "Where are you?" List as many one-sentence answers as you can—about choices, actions, attitudes, regrets, or hurts.

Example: "I've been caught up in trying to be cool. I've been willing to compromise." Or "I'm hurt by my parents' divorce. I've been hiding my pain."

Now make your list. When you're finished, think of God asking the question, "Where are you?" Answer him with something you wrote on your list. Stop after each one and imagine stepping out of hiding and being with God, who longs for you to return to him. Spend some quiet time alone with God.

What's God telling you about where he wants to take you? Finish by writing some of those thoughts.

> *God longs for us to go before him with our souls naked and open to seeing all that we've become trapped in—not so we will be so struck down we can't get up and live, but with the goal that we can now go forward living more fully and passionately, immersed in the things that count.*
>
> (*Eyes Online : Eyes On Life, p. 85*)

three
connection

- Consider some of the ways God has brought people into your life to encourage you. Be prepared to talk about a person or two who has been there for you.
- Choose one of the Bible stories mentioned in this session and read more about it. Imagine yourself meeting Jesus like the person in the story did.

Leader note: For the "Experience It" activity you will need two wheelbarrows (preferably or mostly clean, if possible); two blindfolds; and enough area to create a short obstacle course.

SUZY WANTED TO FIT IN and be liked. At first that meant a little more makeup and tighter clothes. Then she decided to turn things up a notch, to do whatever it took to be cool—even if it meant having sex to get the popular guy. She tried on different "Suzys" as she juggled her time between groups of friends. For a while, she got by with playing the *together* Christian around her youth group and then having another face for the popular crowd at school.

The pressure to keep up that lifestyle soon wore her down. Friendships were based on expectations and lies, and she lost track of who *Suzy* really was. What scared her most was that she cared less and less.

God created Suzy, and each of us, intricately. With a purpose. When we make choices that take us away from those purposes,

What was she doing? Sometimes she felt good in Josh's arms. He seemed to care about her, but it seemed like their whole relationship was about sex. She was getting sick of it. Sick of herself. It left her feeling empty, though she wasn't sure why, given all the talk about how great it was supposed to be. For now she just wanted to get through this night and figure out what she was going to do the next day.
(Seduced By Sex : Saved By Love, p. 133)

nothing feels quite right or real. We might smile and look like we're fine on the outside, but inside we only know emptiness and pain. Something is missing, but we're not sure what. Or if we do know, we're not sure how to get it back.

Like Suzy, you may have made choices to do whatever it takes to go after what you really wanted. The result may have been that you ended up hurting at depths you never thought possible. God wants so much more for you— connections that fully honor who he created you to be, connections that encourage growth, healing, and freedom. Have you experienced that? Through a family member or friend? A taste of one? A glimpse?

Snapshots of Jesus. Here are three.

As early as junior high, CORY'S struggles included depression, thoughts of suicide, and cutting. During that time he also was arrested for use and possession of marijuana. By high school he was having sex regularly. Then his grandmother invited him to church. "The first person I got to know was the worship leader. I respected him because of his music, but he really took me under his wing. He would push me to try new things. Try this instrument, this solo. I'd really never had anyone that invested in me like that. His actions helped me get a feeling for who God might be."

Just one touch was what one woman in Jesus' time hoped for. She had been ill and bleeding for so many years that even the doctors had given up on her (Mark 5:25-34). Rejection, isolation, and weakness darkened her days. Death may not have been far off. But she'd heard of Jesus. Could she risk going out into the streets, possibly in violation of the cultural laws for those who were bleeding in such a way? She had to. She had to find this one man who had healed so many.

You can picture this woman—we are never told her name—cloaking her body and face so she would not be recognized, making her way through the streets, hoping to find Jesus. She wouldn't bother him, wouldn't even let him know she was there. She figured that if she could just touch the edge of his garment, and slip away, somehow she would be healed.

When she found Jesus, crowds were pressing around him. She stepped closer, then closer, then reached, and finally . . . touched him. She felt it, immediately, through her whole body. She felt some sort of power, something moving through her. And then, she was healed. She quietly rejoiced and hoped to leave unnoticed.

But Jesus stopped and asked those around him who had touched him. She couldn't hide. She confessed. Jesus told her, "Daughter, you took a risk of faith, and now you're healed and whole. Live well, live blessed! Be healed of your plague" (Mark 5:34, *The Message*).

This woman demonstrated courageous faith, but Jesus wanted more for her just than a healed body. He wanted connection, he wanted relationship—so he called her daughter. With Jesus, we see this kind of intentional pursuit again and again. God loves each of us that much.

Let's look at another story, of a blind man named Bartimaeus (Mark 10:46-52; Luke 18:35-43). He often begged on the streets, so he knew of Jesus, though he had never met him. Maybe he hoped to, maybe he thought he never would. But one day, among the crowded streets, Jesus came. As soon as Bartimaeus realized who it was, he called out for his help.

Some around him told him to be quiet, but Bartimaeus only grew bolder and more determined. He cried out, "Jesus, Son of David, have mercy on me" (Luke 18:38). Jesus stopped. He could have walked over to Bartimaeus and healed him, or he could have done the same from where he stood and then went on his way. Instead, he did much more.

First, Jesus asked others to bring the blind man to him. Then he had a question for Bartimaeus: "What do you want me to do for you?" (Luke 18:41). This is a great question for all of us to consider. What *do* we want Jesus to do for us? Bartimaeus told Jesus that he wanted to see.

Then Jesus healed him and said that Bartimaeus's faith had made him well. If we dig into the language used here, we find that Jesus meant not only his blindness, but also his soul.

All of Jesus' actions in his encounters, such as these two, point to a desire for deep and lasting connection, with God and with others. Jesus did not heal from a distance, or heal quickly or only in part. He fully engaged in what was happening with this man and involved others

KATIE was abandoned by many people in her life, including her parents. Deep loss, pain, and mistrust caused her to put up walls. But with new friendships that demonstrated Jesus' love, she began to let others in, including God. "I was very resistant. I pushed away people who were trying to help. I wanted them to prove they cared about me. I discovered that there really are people I could depend on. They chose to stick by me and walk through everything with me. That helped me see what a relationship with Christ could be."

As a teen, JUSTIN got into drugs, alcohol, and sex. He made his way back to church and ended up on a mission trip in Mexico. On the second day after dinner, his youth pastor asked to spend some time with him. "I knew what was coming. I told myself, *I'm not going to listen to anything he says.* But when he started talking to me, it was everything I needed to hear, everything I longed to hear. That was when I gave my life to God."

in the healing. And then there was the question: "What do you want me to do for you?" If he saw you in need sitting by the side of the road, he would do all of this for you too. In fact, he does.

The third snapshot focuses on a story involving a paralyzed man and his buddies (Matthew 9:1-13; Mark 2:2-5). These amazing friends heard Jesus was in town, and being the resourceful guys they were, they knew where to find him. They lifted their paralyzed friend onto a cot to carry him to the house where Jesus was, but when they arrived they saw that many others were already there. Small problem: they couldn't get through.

That wouldn't stop these guys. They carried their crippled friend up to the roof, tore off a few tiles, and lowered him right in front of Jesus. Picture it: must have been quite a scene. Mark 2:5 says: "Seeing their faith, Jesus said to the paralyzed man, 'My son, your sins are forgiven.'"

In this snapshot you see the creativity of friendship—guys who did whatever it took to get their friend to Jesus. Jesus noticed this too. He recognized their faith. Amazing friends. Amazing connections.

Relationships that help us know Jesus are of huge importance to God. It's about connecting with him, but it's also about connecting with others who fully honor and encourage who you were created to become.

Suzy, unfortunately, spiraled to dark and lonely places in her life before she realized that her choices and relationships were only hurting her and taking her further from God. But friends and mentors were waiting for her, ready to listen and help. God was there too.

Maybe you've experienced too many painful relationships, and you wonder if it's possible to have strong, life-giving friendships—those that will help you thrive in your faith and take you forward on your journey. Look around. Maybe God has already brought people into your life. They could just be waiting for you to say you are willing.

While Suzy was still cautious about letting people into her world, God was putting options in place for her. Others in her church, including her youth pastor, Martin, had noticed her struggle, and though Suzy's parents didn't attend the same church until later, they began to feel the support Suzy was starting to receive. Sharon, the senior pastor's wife, and Karen were two women who began to reach out to Suzy and her parents. Suzy felt alone, but she wasn't. When she was ready, they'd be there.
(*Seduced By Sex : Saved By Love*, p. 108)

But as for me, I will sing about your power. Each morning I will sing with joy about your unfailing love. For you have been my refuge, a place of safety when I am in distress.

PSALM 59:16, NLT

TOGETHER

/ / Consider It

Talk about how relationships—good or bad, strong or weak—impact our choices and perceptions of ourselves and of God. What have you experienced with the influences of relationships—both helpful and hurtful? What do you do about those who are hurting you?

Talk about what it means to fully honor who God created you to be in ways that encourage growth, healing, and freedom. How can you do that for yourself?

Suzy needed vital relationships to encourage and support her move toward freedom and transformation. She discovered that not all relationships do that. What do you need to look for when searching for supporting relationships that honor where God wants to take you?

In what ways do you personally need courage to go to God and connect with him? What does the story of the woman who touched Jesus' robe tell you about his openness to that connection?

How can you creatively encourage and support others, including those in this group?

The questions Jesus asked were opportunities for the person who came to him to think about what they really wanted or what they were truly thinking. But each question also led the person to a deeper connection with Jesus. Look again at the question he asked Bartimaeus, and then look at two more:

The question Jesus asked Bartimaeus just before he healed him: *What do you want me to do for you?*
Mark 10:46-52; Luke 18:35-43

A question Jesus asked his disciples: *Who do you say that I am?*
Matthew 16:13-17; Mark 8:27-29; Luke 9:18-20

The question Jesus asked Peter after Peter had denied him three times: *Do you love me?*
John 21:15-17

Talk about the deeper invitations and challenges that Jesus is extending as he asks each of these differing questions. What is your personal answer to each question? How does that impact your journey with him?

/ / Experience It

The key for this activity is to work together as a group to decide how you'll accomplish the task and keep the person inside the wheelbarrow. Though this is not a race—initially anyway—it will be great challenge.

Your leader will ask for four volunteers: two who will be carried in the wheelbarrows and two who will do the pushing. Set up a mini-obstacle course around chairs and tables that is identical for both teams. Just one more factor: blindfold both wheelbarrow pushers. The person in each barrow has to call out the directions to the person doing the pushing. (And you may end up with other students shouting, creating an additional obstacle!)

Before you start: make sure you have a safe course. If so, you'll have a blast with this activity. Have a couple of rounds through the course if you can.

Afterward: discuss what was needed. Who needed to communicate? What were people thinking and feeling—the ones in the wheelbarrows, the ones pushing? Talk about how what was experienced can relate to our connections with others and with God, about how crucial it is to both give and receive help in our struggles and journeys.

Just for fun: afterward, have some more fun with wheelbarrow races through the courses.

JUST YOU AND GOD

// A Look Inside

Connections with others fill the pages of your story. Many are vital and transformative for your life and your journey. But maybe you've discovered, like Suzy, that others are hurtful, even destructive. Which ones might be good to walk away from, and what would change if you did?

(This is for personal reflection and names should not be used in your small group.)

Imagine yourself sitting on the road with your own form of spiritual blindness. How would you describe that blindness? What would you ask of Jesus?

Describe your relationship with God as it is today. Given what you've considered and talked about through your small group time, what do you see doing differently to have a stronger connection with him?

What can you do differently in your relationships that will honor who God created you to be?

/ / A Step Deeper

Hold a personal worship time; include songs that specifically invite a deeper connection with God. Bring the volume down a notch, read Scriptures, pray out loud, or spend a few moments in silence, just listening to God. Maybe do some journaling about what God is showing you about your relationship with him or with others.

> God wasn't pushing a bunch of impossible demands on [Suzy]. He was pursuing her. He was after her heart. "That was the first time I ever thought about that," she said. "He loves me? He likes me? He still wants me after all I've done and gone through? How could he? After that I let him pursue me. I knew I wanted in and wanted healing."
>
> (Seduced By Sex : Saved By Love, p. 179)

LET'S TALK : TELLING YOUR STORY

Making sure you have close relationships, people you can talk with and share your story with, may or may not be an easy thing for you. Where do you begin? Let's break it down.

// WHO CAN YOU TALK WITH?

Check with your pastors or your small group leader and see if they have suggestions. Look for someone who is older, of the same sex, and who has a solid relationship with Christ. That means they really know how to live out their faith in practical ways, every day, and through the tough stuff. This person can be someone you enjoy hanging out with, but they also should know how to blend their commitment to Christ into all areas of their life. They won't be perfect, but they should know how to be compassionate, listen well, and know how to challenge you to keep moving forward in your journey.

Remember, you don't have to tell your story the first time you hang out with someone. It's OK to take time to get to know someone and develop that trust first.

/ / HOW WILL YOU TELL YOUR STORY?

Plan an opening sentence or two, a way to introduce your story. For ideas, read through what you've written for some of the "Just You and God" sections.

If it's easier, write it out, read it to your friend, or let them read it.

Give your friend time to respond. It's OK if they seem to need some time to think and be quiet. That's not a bad thing.

Be prepared for follow-up questions, but if a question feels too uncomfortable, tell your friend and talk through why.

Tell them why it was important to share your story. It might be coming out of hiding and letting someone know. It might be that you're ready to ask someone to help you take some of the next steps toward getting out of your traps. It might be the time for you to ask someone to help you grow closer to God, to learn more about him, or to trust him more deeply.

/ / WHAT ABOUT THE NEXT TIMES YOU MEET?

It might take more than a couple of times hanging out to share your story. Other details will come to mind later. As you continue to meet and talk, work together to discover ways to move forward in your growing relationship with God.

And every time you meet doesn't have to be about all the serious stuff; have fun together too. Those times often lead to more trust and more opportunities to talk about new things, including where God is taking you.

four
freedom

- Think about one area of your life where you see God helping you overcome a struggle or helping you grow (or both).
- Look up some of the Scriptures in this session and consider what they mean to you when you think about freedom.
- Bring two oversized shirts, T-shirts, or button-down shirts you can use for "Experience It." Make sure you can put them on over the clothes you'll be wearing.

Leader note: Also needed for this activity will be two stacks of paper (a different color for each stack); duct tape; having extra large shirts for those who forget (or newcomers) is a good idea.

COLIN'S DEPRESSION and struggles with online traps seemed to grow better, or worse, depending on how circumstances were going in his life. Part of that could have been because he kept his battle with pornography secret. But that came out in the open when an online friend figured it out. Admitting it to his youth pastors was the next huge step. He got more help and asked for accountability.

Later Colin attended a retreat and walked away feeling an amazing connection with God. That feeling had faded away after other retreats. He wanted this time to be different. His heart, now determined to be free of the traps, was opened wide to God making a real difference in his life.

Freedom.

What is it and what does it look like played out in your life? Does it feel in reach? Or more elusive, like something slipping from your grasp just when it seemed possible?

John 8:36 tells us that if Jesus sets us free, we are really free. This is certain and true. It has a lot of hope packed into it, but what is the freedom he's talking about? How are we set free?

It's clear from Colin's story, and our own, that experiencing that freedom has to be about more than things going great in our lives, or an amazing experience, or saying we're going to live differently. Those things might help some, but what will it take to get to the freedom that really transforms our lives—with no going back?

MARIUS was consumed with playing competitive online games. Nothing and no one in his life was as important as winning in his virtual world. But he felt God calling him to something more. "I still fought the feeling a little longer. It was a choice God had placed before me, but I felt him say that if I decided to chase after him, I had no idea how amazing it would be. I got on my knees and asked for his forgiveness for placing those games before my relationship with him."

four

"How can you say that we shall be set free?" was a question the Jews asked Jesus (John 8:33). They were offended. They told him they'd never been slaves of anyone, which was not at all true. Two examples were their bondage by the Egyptians and later by the Babylonians. Still, from their perspective, Jesus couldn't possibly talk to *them* about being free. Freedom wasn't something they were in need of.

So with their minds slammed shut, they didn't like what he said next any better. Jesus said: "I tell you the truth, everyone who sins is a slave to sin. Now a slave has no permanent place in the family, but a son belongs forever. So if the Son sets you free, you will be free indeed" (John 8:34-36). His offer to them was for true and full freedom. Some, through God's work in their hearts, did see what Jesus offered as the extravagant, powerful gift that it was (John 6:35-37, 44; Romans 3:24; 1 John 1:9).

But these and others like them? They wanted to kill Jesus, and his message.

Hardened hearts and deeply instilled pride led many to reject Jesus and to rise up against the message of hope he offered. His heart broke over their slavery and blindness to their traps and sin.

He was accused, arrested, and given an unfair trial. Mocking him, they pressed a crown of thorns into his scalp, and he was led to the cross. Laughed at, spat on, humiliated. Whipped, tortured, speared. Broken, wounded, scarred. Executed.

And yet God the Father knew all this was going to happen. It was the only way. From times long before that day, he had decreed that a sacrifice must be given for sin. Jesus, with his death, finished it. Once and for all. (Read John 19:30; Hebrews 9:11-14; 1 Peter 3:18.)

That's love.

One soldier, who witnessed how Jesus breathed his dying breaths, said, "Surely this man was the Son of God!" (Mark 15:39).

Jesus could not be bound. He rose again to life—an assurance for us that not only was he who he said he was, but that the freedom and life he offered was powerful and real. No longer out of reach.

What were his first followers to do with all this? What are we to do with it?

After he rose from the dead, Thomas, one of Jesus' disciples, didn't believe the man standing before him was his Lord. Too much had happened; Thomas was too much in shock and disbelief. But Jesus told him to touch his side, to see the wounds in his hands (John 20:27-29). What a moment that must have been. Jesus, standing there alive, with the wounds he freely took on himself so evident. Doubts melted as Thomas touched the scars, and then Jesus said, "Believe."

Freedom, true freedom, comes from a powerful love relationship with Jesus, an experience like what Thomas knew that day. It's more than a knowledge of who Jesus is as the world describes him and more than simply believing that what he did on the cross is true. It's realizing the hugely personal nature of our traps and sins and what they meant to Jesus as he willingly stretched out his arms to lay on

NICOLE was molested as a child, and then as a teen she became sexually active. She later wished that none of that had happened and regretted treating sex as if it didn't matter. But today she knows God's forgiveness and healing. "God loves me and sees me completely free and washed clean from my past. I pray that God will continue to heal me and mold me to be more like him."

CHRISTINE says her parents didn't teach her values, so media and music became her teachers. Her lifestyle as a teenager consisted of plenty of drinking, partying, and sex. "I would still be living in misery and brokenness every day if it weren't for God. He saved me, literally. My choice to face everything and begin healing was very scary. I was only able to do it by trusting him."

four

that cross. It's realizing the ripples of the effects of our choices in not only the events of the cross but also in our lives today.

And it's realizing that if the Son has set us free, we *are* free. Period. Free to not live in lies any longer.

Believe. Believe it all. And live it—you are no longer a slave of the traps that have held you down, but free.

Colin discovered that without God, sadness over his choices was stripped down to empty regrets, stark consequences, or inward self-despair. God was left out of the picture and Colin felt no sense of healing or freedom. But later a heartfelt realization of his sin, and sorrow over the emptiness and destruction of his traps, brought him to a new place of knowledge and hope.

God's work on the cross, his tears, his love, his sacrifice draws us to a place of newness and surrender. We are changed—not because *we* did anything, but because Jesus gave everything. He gave himself.

As the apostle Paul prayed in Ephesians, what a great thing it would be if we could understand more deeply God's love for us so we could be filled with his goodness (Ephesians 3:16-19). And find true freedom.

He had more to learn and conquer, but he was willing.
The changes he'd made, especially in the last half of his senior
year, were sinking deep. Colin would never be the same.
Looking at that time, he said, "God got ahold of me.
I became a completely different person. I talked to people.
I made new friendships. On top of that, my relationship
with God started to flourish. I was able to worship freely.
I prayed more. I read my Bible. I was starting to become
someone people could look up to, and I really and truly
believe that it was all God."
(Eyes Online : Eyes On Life, p. 214)

It is for freedom that Christ has set us free.
Stand firm, then, and do not let yourselves be
burdened again by a yoke of slavery.

GALATIANS 5:1

TOGETHER

/ / Consider It

At first Colin tried making changes, following what he thought was expected of him—the "rules" of living right. The difference came when he realized that only Jesus could give him the freedom he desperately needed. That relationship set genuine transformation into motion.

What things, people, or situations inspire you to change and leave your traps and struggles behind?

Which motivators for change, and freedom, seem to fade with time or testing? Which seem to last?

What did Christ teach about lasting freedom? How does this relate to you living free in practical ways each day? How are you changed by what he did on the cross?

Share how you have felt your faith is growing. Are there new freedoms you are discovering?

Struggles, traps, setbacks. Sometimes freedom seems far off. But with a plan, you will experience greater freedom and deeper transformation. Consider these "I will" statements for your journey:

I will daily seek and follow God.
Psalm 27:8; Matthew 8:19

I will trust God when I am afraid or weak.
Psalm 4:8; 56:3

I will put my hope in God.
Psalm 71:14

I will remember and think often of God's faithfulness in my life.
Psalm 77:12; 91:10

I will live a life of integrity and faith.
Psalm 101:2; 119:15

Journey transformation: For each of the above, what can you do to take it beyond a statement to specific actions in your life? Think about how those actions will impact your journey.

Take it one decision at a time. Know that God joins you, walks with you, and gives you the strength you need. One of his "I will" statements is, "So do not fear, for I am with you; do not be dismayed, for I am your God. I will strengthen you and help you; I will uphold you with my righteous right hand" (Isaiah 41:10).

/ / Experience It

Read 2 Corinthians 5:17 and Ephesians 4:17-22.

Pass out the paper from one of two stacks to each member in the small group. Write words or phrases that represent the old life and old traps you've personally experienced.

Hand out the second stack of paper. On these sheets, write words or phrases that represent the opposites of the words and phrases you wrote on the other paper. Include where you're headed on your journey, what you see as becoming your new life.

Cut out the words and phrases from the two sheets.

Have your two shirts ready. Use the tape to attach the words representing your old life and traps to one shirt, and then do the same with the words representing your new life on the other shirt.

When everyone has their words taped, put on the clothing that represents the old life. Talk about it: are you feeling comfortable with it or wanting to get that shirt off as soon as possible? Talk about what it feels like, what you want, where you'd like to head.

Now take off that shirt and put on the one that has the words representing the new life. What are some of your thoughts? Considering the words you have on this shirt, what do you feel? What encouragement or challenge is God calling you to?

With the second shirts on, conclude your time by praying for each other and asking God to help you make these things more and more a part of your life.

JUST YOU AND GOD

// A Look Inside

Imagine being free of your traps and also living fully, as God intended. What does this look like within your personal story?

When you consider putting off the old and putting on the new, what is most significant to you? Consider the shirts activity in "Experience It." Invite God to help you with this.

How does your faith impact your view of freedom? How would you describe the strength of your faith at this moment?

Are there specific thoughts, relationships, or situations that seem to be getting in the way of greater faith and freedom? What do you need to know or do to move forward?

Look through the list of "I will" statements under "Journey Transformations." Choose one that you'd like to focus on and write it in your own words. What are some specific actions you can take this week? Ideas:

+ "I will respond _____ to temptation."

+ "I will have _____ as accountability partners/supporters."

+ "I will memorize _____ (verses)."

// A Step Deeper

What makes you feel excited and free? Running? Painting without thought of the finished product? Helping out in a shelter? Choose an activity to do this week, and while you're doing it, ask God to show you more about the freedom he has for you. When you're finished, journal your impressions. Find verses that support your discoveries.

> One thing is for certain: [Colin] sees that God never gave up on him. "Anytime I felt hopeless, or felt like God wasn't there, he was listening and not abandoning me. Putting things in perspective, God was there the whole time."
>
> (*Eyes Online : Eyes On Life*, pp. 215, 216)

five
going deeper

- Skim through this session and select Scriptures that will help you understand more about Joshua's life and battles.
- Consider your own current battles and struggles and how you can begin to invite God to be a part of those.

Leader note: All you'll need for "Experience It" is a Hacky Sack or a small, light ball.

FOR TIFFANY, freedom from sadness and self-destructive choices began to feel in reach, but she wasn't sure what she was supposed to do with the self-hatred and anger that continued to tug her back toward hopelessness. Memories of her father's betrayal through his abuse often darkened her thoughts. Feelings of worthlessness dropped her right back into using self-injury or manipulation of her eating and exercise as a way to find comfort or control.

At church, Tiffany found friendship and support through her youth pastor and his wife. Trust was built, and she began to share her story of abuse and self-destructive behavior. Many hours of time spent with her youth pastor's wife helped her work through the lies and self-hatred. God loved her. She was not worthless. The pull of the old traps of self-injury and self-hatred was strong, but even more powerful was the real freedom she knew she would find through going deeper with God.

Going deeper in your journey is exciting. God works in ways you never imagined. Newness and hope is not only in reach, but

> "I realized how deep God's love was for me.
> A passage of Scripture that I went to is Romans
> 8:31-39. I have learned to cling to these verses.
> I also learned that even when I was angry with
> God, his faithfulness was amazing. Even when
> I didn't feel like he was anywhere in reach in those
> dark moments, he was right there with me,
> and his heart was breaking right alongside
> of mine. He cares that deeply."
>
> —Tiffany

you also see evidence that all of this can change your story, your journey. You feel it—it's changing *you*. That connection to God is real and powerful.

You've also likely discovered that living that relationship out every day isn't always easy. You're thinking more about God. You're reading the Bible and understanding his words more. You're learning about his power, love, and character—even trusting him on deeper levels.

But Satan can work hard and place many obstacles in your way. Questions stir inside you; the hard stuff still happens from day to day. Sometimes you hit those moments that tear into your heart when you've slipped back toward some of the old traps and thoughts. You might feel miserable—more than you ever did before.

Impatience and anger, the struggle to forgive. The pull of traps or friends that you know can take you under. Regrets that you "did it again."

CORY struggled with drugs, depression, cutting, smoking, and sex—some of that even after he became involved in his church's youth group. After attending a festival, he discovered how much more God had for him. "I accepted Christ and I really, really got interested. 'What's this mean?' 'What's next?' I got a study Bible, got into devotions, and that really moved me forward with God. Now I really had something I could turn to that wasn't destructive."

five

Feelings of being lost or bad or worthless or hopeless. Just going through the motions. Tempted to give up.

The changes God is making in you are still happening deep inside—in life-impacting ways. In fact, when you feel the painful conflict between where you want to go and what you chose instead, it could be that you do care and maybe are more sensitive to hearing him. Otherwise you probably wouldn't have noticed.

But what do you do about those moments—and they can seem too many to count—when life is just plain tough? How do you prepare to face the battles and not only make it through, but also get to the other side stronger?

Take a look at Joshua of the Old Testament. Wow, talk about life journeys. A good part of this guy's journey included trekking through a desert wilderness and fighting battles that seemed impossible to win. When we pick up his story in the Bible, he is running for his life, along with the Israelites, escaping the oppression and pursuit of the Egyptian pharaoh and his army.

As the chase takes them to the edge of a sea, trapped with no place to go, Moses, Joshua's leader, reminds all of them, "The Lord himself will fight for you. Just stay calm" (Exodus 14:14, *NLT*). We'll really never know how the Israelites did with being quiet and remaining calm, but we do know God fought for them. In the next few moments, God split apart the sea walls and sent the Israelites walking through to the other side on dry ground. As the enemy army entered the sea in a wild pursuit, the sea crashed back into place, destroying them (Exodus 14:26-31).

Safe. For a while. But the Israelites are quickly in danger again when the Amelekites attack. Joshua, the trusted right-hand man to Moses, is appointed to command the first battle in the desert against the Amelekite forces (Exodus 17:8-14). And he entered that battle having recently witnessed how God's Word was true. God did fight for them. He would again.

Things settled down again, and Joshua was one of twelve men (representing the twelve tribes of Israel) who were sent ahead to spy out the land God said they would claim. Some of the twelve were afraid of what they saw and returned with a report of the unbeatable power of the cities and armies they would face if they went forward. Joshua and another man, Caleb, instead offered a very unpopular report. Most wanted to believe it was impossible, but Joshua and Caleb had confidence. They had faith in God that he would give them the victory, that God would once again help them fight the battles. The two men stood by their convictions even though others became so angry they wanted to stone them to death.

God decided to give them all a few years to work through their attitudes. We'll jump ahead a few pages in the story, past forty years of desert wanderings and to a new generation of Israelites who have replaced the old. The Israelites were at that place again, considering the prospect of going in and fighting for the land God had reserved for them. Moses had died, and God told Joshua to go for it.

Joshua was forty years older. Would he take

Through the mentoring of others, KATIE, who was abandoned by many significant people in her life, grew to trust God and to love spending time with him. "He's a part of every moment of my day. Studying God's Word was a very valuable piece in my healing, and it continues to be. I can see why God calls people to do certain things, and the way he works, and how that applies to me today. It's important to me to have that connection with what's on the pages of Scripture. It makes everything come alive."

ANDREW struggled with online addictions, which included countless hours in front of the computer. Pornography was a struggle. He knows the battle strategy. "There's a lot of power you're calling on when you pray. God makes it really clear in a lot of Scriptures that he wants you to use that kind of power to your advantage. He will be there to assist you, not in any way that you want, but in the best way that you need."

five

on the challenge and the battles ahead? God assured him that he would again be with him in the battles ahead. They would fight for a huge territory and face powerful armies, but they would gain all the land he promised them—one that was spacious and good, described as "flowing with milk and honey" (Exodus 3:8). Abundance. Freedom. Joy. All good gifts from God.

To be successful, God also gave them a few important pointers. He told them to be strong and very courageous—several times in the first chapter of Joshua, in fact, they are given these words. And he tells them to always keep in their minds his words written down for them, to do all that they say and never depart from them. *Then* they are assured success.

And there was Joshua, pointing the way with leadership and courage, telling the people to prepare and to go. They fought and won the battles, and they claimed all the land God had promised.

You fight battles too, but those you're most familiar with today take on a different shape. Journey battles aren't fought on fields of unknown lands with swords and armor, but they are just as real, just as important.

And God is just as present in those battles.

You're going along fine. Then the battles come. The enemies of your heart are in hot pursuit, hoping to weaken you, discourage you, and most of all stop you from getting to that place where you can experience all that God has in mind for you.

God's words written down for an ancient civilization are every bit as much for you today. So, what should be your battle strategy?

Know the Lord himself will be with you in the battles. Jesus is the warrior who fights for you, the one to take with you into your battles, to trust your life with. He is mighty God (Isaiah 9:6), deliverer (Romans 11:26), life-giving spirit (1 Corinthians 15:45), and the shepherd and guardian of our souls (1 Peter 2:25, *NLT*).

Be strong. Be very courageous (Ephesians 6:10-18; 1 Corinthians 10:13; 2 Corinthians 12:9, 10).

Remember God's words written down for you. Keep them in your mind, keep them close at hand. Don't forget them. Live them out—no matter what (Psalm 119:15, 16; 2 Corinthians 10:5).

Through her doubts and healing, Tiffany clung to God and to his words. When battles and discouragement threatened, she moved forward in growing trust, believing that he was bringing her deeper into a relationship with him and to a place of fullness, freedom, and joy.

> *"Discipleship was one of the most beneficial things for me. My youth pastor's wife made me aware through encouragement and Bible study that I was a living a defeated life by believing the lies Satan was attacking me with. I spent time in God's Word regularly. It wasn't enough to just read it. I needed to fully trust every word of it, apply it to my life, and live it out. It's incredible to look back and remember what God has brought me from. Just incredible."*
>
> *—Tiffany*

The Lord will guide you always; he will satisfy your needs in a sun-scorched land and will strengthen your frame. You will be like a well-watered garden, like a spring whose waters never fail.

Isaiah 58:11

five

TOGETHER

/ / Consider It

Tiffany battled the memories and pain of abuse and the resulting self-hatred. She longed for the answers and the strength to get back on track. She turned to others who could help her know the truth about God, and she fought hard to know him personally. What battles are you facing right now?

Talk about battle strategies that will move your journey toward freedom.

Joshua's strategies were linked to a strong trust in God. He remembered what God had done in the past and was fully confident God was with them. What have you experienced of God's actions and his faithfulness in your life?

How can knowing and remembering God's faithfulness in your life help you go deeper with him and strengthen your trust?

The enemies of your heart are in pursuit; one battle strategy is to know who or what those enemies are. Talk about the enemies of your heart. How can you prepare yourself so you're not caught off guard?

Choose one or more of the categories below and explore those verses. Consider how God will fight in these battles for you.

Preparation for the worst enemy of all:
Ephesians 6:10-18; 1 John 2:14

The battle is bigger than you think. How will you fight?

The battle for confidence and sufficiency:
2 Corinthians 3:4, 5; 12:9, 10

You can win this battle. But what will be the source from which you draw your strength?

Finding unlimited possibilities for your journey:
Ephesians 3:14-20; Philippians 4:13

How will God work with you in all that is ahead?

Companions—surprising ones—of the strengths you'll need for your battles:
Isaiah 30:15; 40:29-31

What will take you deeper in your trust of God?

/ / Experience It

Start this game by tossing around the Hacky Sack or ball. Everyone has to catch and throw, however, with the opposite hand of the one they normally use. After a bit of this, talk about the importance of using your strengths and working in the way that God made you. (And, if you've got some great Hacky Sackers, have everyone kick the sack around; talk about how teamwork must be a strength in this activity.)

Next, a discovery of strength. God is your source of strength. He is your sufficiency and there when you're weak, but he also created you uniquely with strengths, gifts, and abilities to use to serve and to honor him.

+ What have others pointed out that you do well?

+ What do you enjoy or find easy to do—to the point that you can't understand why others can't do it?

+ What do your answers to these two questions tell you about yourself? What are some of your strengths?

Next, focus on one person at a time. Everyone in your small group should tell that person one thing he or she sees as a strength in them. Try not to repeat. End this time praying for each other—that the strengths that God has given each of you will be an encouragement and will be used to take your journey farther and deeper.

JUST YOU AND GOD

/ / A Look Inside

When you face battles or feel discouraged, do you picture yourself alone or with God alongside, fighting for you? How does each perspective affect your efforts?

Battle plans help prepare us. What have you discovered that can become a part of your battle plan for your freedom journey?

Take a few moments to think about, maybe even list, the changes you've made and the ways you see God working. Describe your goal of freedom at this point in your journey. How can you take it deeper?

God had an amazing place planned for the Israelites, and though they would have to fight battles to get there, it would be worth it. Where do you see God taking you in your journey? What does he want you to fight for?

// A Step Deeper

List the strengths you discovered during this session. Write other strengths you see or just things that you like about yourself. Ask God to show you how these might be a part of his encouragement to be strong and courageous. Choose several from your list to think about as you go through each day this week. What are ways you can use them to do something creative or helpful for others? Journal about what you discover.

Johan said: "I have found that my actions are the outworking of what I've decided in my mind. So when a thought or a temptation presents itself to my mind, I stop right there and confess, 'God, I cannot overcome this in my own strength. Please put my sinful nature to death and empower me to obey you.' Taking these thoughts captive and making them obedient to Christ is pivotal."

(Eyes Online : Eyes On Life, pp. 179, 180)

GROUNDING : DEEPENING BIBLE STUDY & PRAYER

Spending solid time digging into the Bible and taking time to pray are two activities that ground you in the faith and can hugely impact your journey. In fact, doing these two things can transform you. A lot of people see these two activities as optional. God would rather you not do either out of burdened obligation or drudgery, but he does want you to use them as gifts and amazing opportunities. As you do, they'll naturally become an important part of each day—as vital to you as breathing. Here are some ideas for going deeper.

/ / BIBLE STUDY

Spend time praying before you study. Ask God to give you an open heart to see what he wants to show you during this time.

Choose a book of the Bible to read throughout the week, or use Scriptures from this study that are about a particular topic.

Write out questions you'd like to think about each time you read. Suggestions: What does this show me about God's character? What does it tell me about my journey? What is God wanting me to see about participating in his unfolding story? How will I make it practical for my life today?

Journal what you discover. Make lists or write prayers to God as a response.

LIVE FREE JOURNEY

Choose Scriptures that specifically encourage you in your journey; memorize them.

Ask someone to help you learn how to use resources for getting deeper into the language, meaning, culture, and history behind the Scriptures. These will help you more accurately see what God might have meant by various difficult passages, or to answer questions you have about him and your journey.

/ / PRAYER

Since prayer is a conversation with God, spend time both listening and talking to God.

In listening, you can begin by reading a Scripture that you have found meaningful and then asking God to help you understand it at a greater depth.

Take time to be quiet and think about God being with you: present in this moment, present in your struggles, present when you're doing the ordinary things of a day—always with you.

Sit with him in quiet when you want to experience his peace.

If you like to sing, offer to God a praise or worship song you already know, or sing your own words and make them into a prayer.

Include in your prayers: praising and thanking God for who he is and what he's done; confessing your sins and weaknesses and asking for forgiveness; praying for help to forgive others; asking for help, wisdom, and provision for yourself or for others; dedicating yourself and your day to him and what he wants to accomplish.

Consider the prayer Jesus asked us to pray in Matthew 6:9-13. Look at the different parts of it, then turn it into a personal prayer from you.

Turn Scriptures that are meaningful to you into prayers.

Remember, you can pray anytime during the day. It will keep you connected to God.

six
deeper still

- Spend a few minutes thinking about where God might be taking your life.
- Read about the prophet Jeremiah in Jeremiah 1:1-10.

A STORY IN GOD'S HANDS unfolds in amazing ways. A life is changed, renewed, and moved forward. There is a deepening of purpose.

The part of Suzy's journey that took her down the painful path of false intimacy had pricked her heart with sadness and regret, but also left her with a growing passion to reach out to others. Her hope is that others won't experience what she did, and if they have, that they would discover that God has so much more for them. "They need to know there's hope, healing, forgiveness—life after the state they've been in, newness," she says.

Suzy found that relationship of hope, healing, and forgiveness with Christ. Today she is married to Shane and loves being a mom. She continues to open her heart to God's healing and transformation, and she sees the fruit of his work in her as he brings others to her, one at a time, who need to hear his message of hope.

The writer of Psalm 1 wrote about someone who has walked away from the traps and places or people who bring him down.

> *Today, even in the first moments of spending time with Suzy and Shane, you witness the love they have for each other. Shane said, "There have been huge obstacles and deep valleys because of the way Suzy's past affects her now, but when the only language you speak is hope and love, then there is no other way.*
> *It all comes back to Christ—it always does.*
> *We are beautiful because he loves us."*
> (Seduced By Sex : Saved By Love, p. 222)

He's excited about God's words, which often come to mind day and night. This person, the psalmist wrote, "is like a tree planted by the streams of water, which yields its fruit in season and whose leaf does not wither. Whatever he does prospers" (Psalm 1:3).

In this poetic image, a gardener has moved the tree from where it was in danger of destruction and intentionally planted it in the rich soil by streams of water. Here it will never lack what it needs to grow and its roots will go deep and strengthen. The result is fruit, season after season, and continual and healthy growth. It doesn't wither. In contrast, it prospers.

This is not only a description of a tree. It can be *you*—your story, your journey. You now see the beginnings of being like the tree planted by the streams. You will experience even more as you go deeper still in living out that vital connection to God.

CORY'S experiences with mentors—his youth pastor and music pastor—inspired him. He is currently a youth ministry major and his desire is to make a difference in the lives of teens. "I see how my pastors treated me and what made me feel good. Teens need to know they're special, someone cares. You ask how they're doing and you sit down and really listen. You follow up. This is really important to them."

God will take your faith, your freedom, your journey to the next level—toward a lifestyle of transformation.

Someone who took his journey to the next level is Jeremiah. He was a young man who became one of God's prophets and stepped into a life and work that wasn't easy, but extremely life-transforming for himself and many others.

Let's listen in on the day God first showed up to talk to Jeremiah about what would become his life's calling. God began the conversation with a little history, saying, "Before I formed you in the womb I knew you, before you were born I set you apart; I appointed you as a prophet to the nations" (Jeremiah 1:5).

Wow. God had set in place powerful plans for Jeremiah before he even took his first breath. At the time God said those words, Jeremiah, probably in his early twenties, considered himself "too young" (Jeremiah 1:6, NLT). In his mind, there was no way he could be a prophet. It just wasn't happening. He didn't see himself as a bold speaker.

Like a gentle father-mentor teaching and encouraging his son, God patiently showed Jeremiah what he should do. "'Do not say, "I am only a child." You must go to everyone I send you to and say whatever I command you. Do not be afraid of them, for I am with you and will rescue you,' declares the Lord. Then the Lord reached out his hand and touched my mouth and said to me, 'Now, I have put my words in your mouth. See, today I appoint you over nations and kingdoms to uproot and tear down, to destroy and overthrow, to build and to plant'" (Jeremiah 1:7-10).

God's passion for his broken and lost people took root in Jeremiah's heart, as we see through his words in Jeremiah 4:19:

"Oh, my anguish, my anguish! I writhe in pain. Oh, the agony of my heart! My heart pounds within me, I cannot keep silent. For I have heard the sound of the trumpet; I have heard the battle cry." The young man, who felt he could not speak, now could not keep silent. Not surprisingly, Jeremiah became known as the "weeping prophet."

Yes, the messages Jeremiah proclaimed as a prophet would be tough, but God did not push him out the door with a good-luck-see-ya-later shove. He was always there as Jeremiah spoke the difficult truth to people who had abandoned their creator and Lord. He was there as the prophet stood up to a cruel and ungodly king (Jeremiah 22:13-19); as another king, put in place by the Babylonians, ignored his messages from God (Jeremiah 37:1, 2); and as he endured several imprisonments (Jeremiah 32, 37, 38). Jeremiah always kept in mind what he knew God would bring—a promise of wholeness, forgiveness, and healing, and a people who would turn toward God with hearts that would seek to know him well (Jeremiah 31:31-34).

Through her ministry with teen girls, TIFFANY has spoken to many who are struggling in many areas of their lives. Most of all, she wants them to know there is someone who really cares about them. "I want them to ultimately find freedom in Christ. I want them to know his never-ending love and forgiveness and know the extent of their worth to him."

MARIUS, who at one time was completely immersed in online gaming, has many goals, including wanting to start a ministry in his home country, South Africa. "I want to spend time in God's Word daily and know him more. I want to see people the way Jesus sees them, and love them the way Jesus loves them. My goal is to preach the gospel to the city of Johannesburg and reach out to the homeless and poor in the city."

That's a glimpse of Jeremiah's journey. How about yours?

What is next for you in your journey may also be something that God has had in mind for you. It is certain he has set you apart—by calling you out of darkness into light (John 12:46; Acts 26:18; 1 Thessalonians 5:5; 1 Peter 2:9, 10). He also has called you to hope, to holiness, and to a life that exhibits fullness and power (1 Peter 1:3; Ephesians 1:18; 1 Peter 1:14-16; John 10:10; 2 Peter 1:3).

A transformed life is God's work not only in you but *through* you as you move into the possibilities of making a difference in your home, church, and community. As with Jeremiah, your age doesn't matter. Step into what God has placed before you. He will be with you.

Where do you begin? Always by living close to Jesus. Stay connected to him and to those who know him well. Look at his words, at his life. Talk to him—often, as much as you can. Pray for a heart to serve and love as he did.

Know that purpose is very much a part of the way God made things, and therefore you have purpose: "For everything, absolutely everything, above and below, visible and invisible, rank after rank after rank of angels—everything got started in him and finds its purpose in him" (Colossians 1:16, *The Message*).

Look at the uniqueness in how he has made you—your interests, your abilities, your creativity. What will you do with those? Dream and then know that God, through the work he is doing within you, will do far more than you can imagine (Ephesians 3:20).

You haven't reached the end of your journey. It's only beginning.

Shane and Suzy's hearts are set toward being in ministry together. Shane hopes to attend a seminary and teach Bible classes in a church or on a college campus. Suzy wants to work with teens and young women and— anytime it may help—share her story.
(Seduced By Sex : Saved By Love, p. 223)

Commit to the Lord whatever you do,
and your plans will succeed.

PROVERBS 16:3

TOGETHER

/ / Consider It

Suzy, Jackie, Colin, Mike, and Tiffany have experienced amazing movement in their lives that was directed by God— "fruit in its season," you might say. They experienced things like productivity in work, willingness to be available to one hurting individual, and ministry and hearts of passion like Jeremiah's. God has been working in your life too. What are the beginnings of the fruit you are seeing?

For any of these individuals, for Jeremiah, and for the one the psalmist spoke of, daily connection with God was crucial. Talk about how that works in your life as you seek to take what you've learned into transforming commitment and action.

What resources do you need and what questions do you need answered in order to take commitment and action beyond this study and into your home, church, and community?

What is rooted deeply in your life right now, and what still needs strengthening?

How do you see your journey steps as becoming a lifestyle of transformation? Talk about the many possibilities, including your dreams, for your journey ahead.

When we nurture a mind-set focused on God's unfolding purposes and plans, we're more likely to make choices that will inspire, encourage, and support transforming action. Think about how God can help you with:

A mind that's set on being all that he has called you to be:
John 10:10; Ephesians 1:18; 1 Peter 1:3; 1:14-16; 2 Peter 1:3

What is one way God sees you that you want to consider more often?

A mind set on thinking about what is good:
Psalm 143:5; Philippians 4:8, 13; Colossians 3:1-3

What's a specific way you will *think* differently about this day?

A mind set on actions that honor who God created you to be:
Romans 6:5; 2 Timothy 2:22

What new action can you take beginning today?

A mind set on eternity:
Psalm 16:11; 2 Corinthians 4:17, 18; 1 John 2:25

What's your hope for eternity, and how will that impact today, the next day, and the next?

/ / Experience It

For this activity you'll create a journey statement, which is something like a mission statement. Keep in mind that you will likely change and refine this as you try new things in life and continue to grow closer to God. For now, though, what you create will begin to reveal the passion God may already be placing in your heart.

I want my journey with God to be characterized by: _____ (fill in descriptive words and thoughts from Scriptures that have been meaningful for your growth)

I want to grow deeper in: _____ (the identity or qualities he is creating in you)

I will grow deeper by: _____ (use words or phrases describing the ways you want to go deeper in what God is doing in you)

I have a passion for: _____ (use specific action words or phrases that describe your passions and ways you can serve others)

My passion would be used with: _____ (the specific group of people God might be calling you to reach or to serve)

Write your journey statement in a way that makes the most sense to you. Don't worry about what others are writing. Make it yours. Make it reflect what God is doing—uniquely—in you.

An example: *I want my journey with God to be characterized by compassion, depth, and holiness. As I grow deeper in becoming more like Christ, a child of light, I want to live more closely to Jesus, more freely and fully, so that I will receive and give challenges and encouragement for a vital and genuine relationship with Jesus. I specifically want to do this with families and teens.*

Finish by sharing your journey statements with each other. Pray for God to continue to work in your lives and bring about his plans and purposes for you. You might even create a time of dedication. Play worship music and have group members tape their journey statements to a large cross.

JUST YOU AND GOD

// A Look Inside

As he did with Suzy, when God works in your heart you begin to see the uniqueness of how he made you, including the possibilities of an unfolding future story with him. What has he helped you discover about yourself and about your future story?

Spend a few minutes dreaming more—even beyond what you did in this session's "Experience It." Make sure you answer this question: what are your passions?

What are some specific ways you'll plan to grow deeper in hope, holiness, and a life that displays God's fullness and power? Write out the possible action steps that come to mind.

How will you use your strengths and your journey statement as part of this plan?

/ / A Step Deeper

Think a few years down the road. Write out a prayer to God about your unfolding story. Think about your journey statement, your passions, how you want to grow deeper, what you'd like see change in the days, months, and years ahead. Use Scriptures that have great meaning for you. You might consider writing out one final statement, a commitment statement to God—what specifically will you do to keep moving toward him and the freedom he has in mind for you?

Enjoy the journey! Live free!

Draw me close and deepen my commitment to you. Prepare me for a future of serving you and honoring you in every way . . .

(*A prayer from Seduced By Sex : Saved By Love, p. 226*)

Your journey and relationship with God becomes a lifestyle of transformation by living it out . . . every day. Thinking about God and how you're living moves from something you're aware of once in a while, to something you consider each day, to becoming a powerful daily part of your life. You're living deeper, fuller, freer.

/ / WAYS TO LIVE IT OUT:

- Stay connected to mentors and disciplers who know God well and will encourage a deep, growing relationship with Jesus (2 Timothy 2:22).

- If you need accountability for some of your traps and struggles, be willing to ask someone who will help you be accountable and who can help you to grow more and more dependent on God for the tough moments (Isaiah 26:3, 4).

- Keep seeking God by spending time with him through prayer and reading his words. Ask him to increase your desire for these moments (Psalm 42:2; 63:1; 119).

- Examine your life and see if there are ways you can more fully engage in the life God is calling you to (Psalm 139:23, 24).

- Watch for ways to use the strengths, gifts, and passions God has placed in you—in your home, in your church, and in your community (Mark 12:30, 31).

- Find ways to share what God is doing in your life. Don't keep it quiet. Celebrate it (Psalm 30:11, 12).

resources
for leaders

Here are some general and specific ideas for making your small groups great.

/ / Small Group Dynamics

Set a schedule for the sessions. Be as consistent as possible with meeting dates and times. This shows your commitment and will in turn impact the participants' ability to stay engaged in the study and in what God is doing in their lives.

Carefully consider the location. What's most conducive to taking the study to heart as well as providing a comfortable place for people to open up and share with the group?

Given the nature of the personal sharing and discussion in this kind of study, consider the group size you envision and whether you will add members once you begin. If not, and if more people are interested after you begin, you can either start a new, separate group or wait to start a new six-week session after this one ends.

Set up mentoring and discipleship partners for interested participants. Because the topics in this study are heavier than many studies, it could be extremely important for some, or nearly all, to meet regularly with mature individuals who have strong relationships with Christ. You should make a priority of ensuring that guys meet with guys and girls with girls. One-on-one time will give your participants an opportunity to work through the struggles and questions they might have about their personal stories and journeys and also help ground them in their growing relationship with Christ. (See "One-On-One" in this resource section for more on this.)

/ / Using the Session Material

This is purposely *not* a fill-in-the-blank study. It is designed to engage the group members and encourage them to interact with the material, each other, you, and (most of all) God. The material, and you as a leader, may offer information they don't know, but the questions, discussions, and interactions are crucial for deepening their personal awareness of what God is doing in their lives and who he is inviting them to become.

Anticipate and be ready to discuss the tough questions. Allow the discussion to lead participants to discover the true God and what he calls them to, instead of formulating misleading, "made up" versions of what faith is.

As you prepare generally and for each session, pray for the individuals in the group. Ask God to show you how you can use this study time to encourage and challenge each one personally.

During discussions, *focus less on telling and more on asking good questions* to encourage thinking and discussion. Be purposeful about moving questions and discussion toward personal action beyond your meeting times.

Bring in other appropriate Scriptures, stories, or questions that you know would be helpful to the individuals in your group. Work relevant issues into the discussion.

Be flexible, and strike a prayerful balance between where the group seems to need to spend more time and getting through all the material. Don't feel a need to cover every point, every verse.

Consider incorporating other short, meaningful periods of time: singing praise and worship songs, praying for each other, or other types of group activities.

| | Using the Live Free Series

Read the Live Free series and be familiar with Jackie, Suzy, and Colin's stories, and the stories of others included in the series, if possible. Incorporate additional stories into the study as you see them fitting a particular need or direction of study.

Consider using the support person tips offered throughout the Live Free books to encourage or help individuals in your small group. Another option is the Bible study sections near the end of each chapter in the Live Free books; these can be used to bring in other Bible references and stories as appropriate. (And still another option is choosing more questions or activities for your group study from those at the end of the Live Free book chapters.)

Be aware of group members who would benefit from reading one of the Live Free books. Recommend the appropriate one, or better yet, give them a copy. Keep a dialogue going, giving them an opportunity to talk through their own stories and questions as they read.

Check out the "Live Free Guide," which follows on the next page; it cross-references the Live Free books with this study.

The questions and issues of the group participants and this study are wider than the issues of self-injury, false intimacy, or online addictions, but you can use the stories and material in these three books to talk about issues either specifically or generally.

STW—*Scars That Wound : Scars That Heal—*
A Journey Out of Self-Injury

SBS—*Seduced By Sex : Saved By Love—*
A Journey Out of False Intimacy

EOL—*Eyes Online : Eyes On Life—*
A Journey Out of Online Addictions

| | Session One : Journey

STW   Getting God in the Picture, pp. 34-36

STW   One Tough Step at a Time, pp. 87-89

SBS   I Want, pp. 34-36

SBS   Big Picture Living, pp. 53-55

Note: selections under Story can also be
included for the Journey session.

| | Session Two : Story

STW   Jackie's story, The Hiding Begins, pp. 23-32

STW   Jackie's story, Help Me Feel Normal, Secrets
Buried Deep, Out in the Light, pp. 39-51

STW   Jackie's story, Why Couldn't She Just Stop?, Dumping
the Confusion, Messages You Can Trust, pp. 55-69

STW   Jackie's story, Losing Hope, Never Alone, pp. 71-80

/ / Session Three : Connection

| | Session Four : Freedom

| | Session Five : Going Deeper

/ / Session Six : Deeper Still

This study time can be just another time-filler that fades after a few weeks, or it can be life-transforming. As a leader, one way to make it the better of those two options is to offer an opportunity for one-on-one, ongoing mentoring and discipleship during the sessions.

If you have time to connect individually, great! More than likely, you'll need to recruit others who have time and a heart for teens. You can also work alongside those in your small group to help them find someone who will mentor or disciple them. In "Let's Talk—Telling Your Story," they'll find a few tips to consider when selecting someone.

Be willing to help them make a change if things aren't working out for any reason.

| | Tips and Ideas

Meet weekly at a time that works for each person and commit to making it work. Reschedule only if it's unavoidable, and then, if possible, set a new time during that same week.

Use at least part of the time to talk about any questions or thoughts he has about the sessions.

Ask how things are going for her on a close-to-daily basis, if possible. (Talk at least a couple of times during the week.)

Be willing to let him talk about whatever is on his mind, and listen well.

Each week incorporate a new challenge that will take her deeper in her relationship with God. Use ideas from the study sessions or from the Live Free books.

Use Scripture naturally in conversation. It's great for him to see how relevant God's Word is.

If accountability is needed on some level, talk about how it would work best for both of you.

Be a strong role model for her by being honest and willing to grow personally and spiritually.

Pray for him, and help him to begin to pray too.

End every conversation, whether in your meeting time or in passing, with some form of encouragement.

So the Live Free Journey group has ended and you had no real plans for continuing to meet after the sessions. But the energy was great, people were engaged, and some (or many) are looking for more direction or simply desire to continue the group relationships. Here are some things to keep in mind or ideas to pursue.

Know where each of the group participants is in his or her journey as you end the group. Have a conversation with each to explore how to keep moving forward and growing deeper. Get them involved in those strategies.

Network your group members with strong, supportive people who can commit to encouraging them on a regular basis.

Create an ongoing Live Free group. Give it your own name and identity. Plan to meet at least monthly to continue encouraging participants to live out their journeys of freedom.

Give participants resources to strengthen their relationship with God. Enhance their ability to get to know him more deeply through prayer and studying Scripture.

Continue to involve them in ministry. Encourage serving and using their strengths and gifts.

Always keep in mind that transformation is a lifestyle. We all need continued encouragement, support, and challenge to keep any new lifestyle commitments going. It's vital to nurture what God began to do in people's lives during these six sessions.

Seduced by Sex : Saved by Love
23964

Eyes Online : Eyes On Life
23965

Scars That Wound : Scars That Heal
23963

DESIGNED TO HELP TEENS AND YOUNG ADULTS OVERCOME STRUGGLES AND ADDICTIONS

Check out these three titles that can help you break free from the past and make the choices needed to take hold of the authentic love God offers.